Iron
of the
Dragon's
Touch
Secrets of
Breaking Power

Iron Hand
of the
Dragon's Touch
Secrets of
Breaking Power

MASTER HEI LONG

PALADIN PRESS
BOULDER, COLORADO

Iron Hand of the Dragon's Touch
Secrets of Breaking Power
by Master Hei Long
Copyright © 1987 by Master Hei Long

ISBN 0-87364-434-4
Printed in the United States of America

Published by Paladin Press, a division of
Paladin Enterprises, Inc., P.O. Box 1307,
Boulder, Colorado 80306, USA.
(303) 443-7250

Direct inquiries and/or orders to the above address.

Contents

Introduction

Breaking skills may very well be the most coveted aspect of the martial arts, perhaps even beyond the applied technical abilities for self-defense. In demonstrations, observers will be more impressed by breaking than by a smooth, effective technique, even if the break is a relatively simple one. There is a mystique surrounding breaking skills that, like any other science, can be broken down to a simple formula once the stage presence is removed. This is not to take away from the complexities involved, because they are certainly there, but a methodical, knowledgeable approach to gaining the proper skill can and will put that same awesome power into your hands and feet. Once there is a method established and adhered to, it is just a matter of time and patience. To be an accomplished expert in breaking also requires the one element that few people have. It is the final ingredient that determines whether an individual will be a mere practitioner or a champion in his endeavor. It is the one ingredient that is a common factor to every champion in every competitive field: an unyielding determination. Without determination, you will not make it past the first ninety days of training. Although the method is here before you, it will be meaningless if you are not determined to accomplish the task and

1

achieve the skill. Set your goals before you start, and decide now that you are going to spend the time training regardless of how many catastrophes come into your life. Separate your life totally from the time and days you set up for training. The conditioning process will get discouraging at times, and at other times it may even get boring. Keep your mind on the light at the end of the tunnel; it is the long-term accomplishment you are seeking, and it is there waiting for a champion to claim it.

Chapter 1

░░░░░░░░░░░░░░░░░░░░░░░░░░░░░░░

The Physics
of Breaking

Regardless of the art you study, be it a martial art, gym-
nastics, or even sculpting, the greater the foundation of
knowledge you have in the subject, the more likely you are
to succeed in mastering that art. Although it is only one of
many facets of the martial arts, breaking requires no less of
a basic understanding. There is much more involved here
than simply callousing your hands and feet and building up
enough power to overcome a chosen target. There are thou-
sands of good black belts in this country who quickly ended
their careers in breaking because they accelerated their
training beyond what their bodies were able to adjust to in
the time spent, and there are just as many who damaged
their hands and feet simply because of the lack of knowledge
of the anatomy of the weapons they were developing. The
anatomy of each weapon you will be training is discussed
in Chapters Two and Three. In this chapter we are going to
try to reach an understanding of the physics of breaking
based on the teachings of two men out of history, the
physicist Sir Isaac Newton, and the Greek philosopher
Pyrrho. A look at their teachings should give you an
understanding of how your body is going to react to your
breaking efforts, and from this understanding will come

wisdom in the art of breaking which in all probability will determine whether you succeed or fail.

Pyrrho lived from 365 B.C. to 295 B.C. His was the first philosophy centered in skepticism. His teaching was essentially this: all terms of judgment are relative. Unless a defined starting point for reasoning can be established, no criterion of judgment can be valid. What is heavy to one man will be light to another, and in the study at hand, what is hard to one man may be soft to another. Our first learning from Pyrrho's teaching is that where you start in terms of target density or how hard you are able to hit a practice block is going to be determined by your individual body structure and strength. You may build a training block and work on it for six months and still not be able to hit it full power, whereas someone else who has never trained in breaking before may be able to hit that same training block full power with no pain or injury. This does not mean you are training improperly, nor does it mean that you should start hitting the block as hard as you can regardless of how much it hurts. Allow your body to develop at its own pace. If you overload an electrical circuit, it is going to burn up or shut down at a safety switch. Your body is going to do the same thing, but it will speak to you in terms of pain and structural damage. Once you have injured an area of the hand or foot in training, it could be as long as a month or even a year until you can resume training again. How fast you develop your weapons is of no significance. Your body can only recover as fast as its natural ability allows it to recover and be ready for the next training session. True, you must be prepared to endure some physical discomfort and pain, and only you can determine where the stopping point is, but set your standards by your knowledge and experience, not by what another practitioner is capable of doing. As long as you are making progress, care not for your immediate abilities. Steady progress will ensure success in the long run.

Again, Pyrrho's skepticism is a noteworthy teaching in terms of relativity. When I completed *Dragons Touch*, I wanted to add a chapter to it that would give an approximate weight force to apply to anatomical targets to cause a certain bone to break, for example, or to traumatize a nerve complex. I wanted this same impact force in pounds per square inch in numerical figures for one-inch boards. What I was trying to establish was a basic formula that would allow a student to be able to determine whether he had the ability to snap a knee joint with a crossing side kick by being able to break a certain number of boards with the same kick. I intended to take an average man, determine the strength of each area of the body and give an approximate weight force to apply to each pressure point, and give a parallel in boards. Had this been possible, a certain number of boards being broken with a certain type of kick or blow would tell the student he was capable of damaging that specific area, and allow the student to practice and develop the strikes accordingly. A rather long study ended in a conversation with a professor at the University of Florida where I was told that water content determines the strength of boards, and other variables that are too numerous to mention here determine the strength of bones and other areas of the body. Even in ten men of the same height and weight, the variables were too great to give a safe average. As for the strength of wood, a single five-foot section of a two-by-four was cut into five one-foot sections and tested for strength in an experiment. Each section, although it had been cut from the same five-foot piece, varied in strength as much as 35 percent. Pyrrho could not accept a judgment unless he could first establish a defined starting point. This same principle applies in your training. Your starting point is relative, and your rate of progress will be relative. Because water content determines the strength of boards and bricks and other variables determine the strength of the body structure, a careful self-study and awareness will be necessary to train progressively without injury. Never use chemicals or drugs to numb an area you are going to train or break with. Stay in tune with your body at all times. If you are training with a partner, do not let his progress influence the intensity of your training, beyond drawing a little courage to endure the pain. Be aware of how much pain you are taking; too much courage will reverse what progress you have made.

Summarily, Pyrrhonian reasoning teaches us that how hard we strike targets in the initial stages of training must be determined by the individual who is training, not by on-lookers or in terms of pounds per square inch. It teaches us that no two bodies will start with the same strength or progress at the same rate. If your training partner is punching through four inches of wood in six months and you are not yet able to hit your training block with full power, do not attempt to keep up with him. This is how injuries occur. Let your body do its job in making the adjustments to the demand you are placing on it, and let it do so at its own pace. This point cannot be stressed enough, and as we go on now to the study of reaction forces by the theory of Sir Isaac Newton, the accompanying graphic illustrations should further caution you on pushing too hard in your training and give you a good understanding of exactly what happens when an accelerated body weapon makes contact with a target.

The physicist Sir Isaac Newton needs no formal introduction. His teachings and theories are taught in American schools at the elementary level. Of particular interest to us here and now is his third law of motion that states concisely that for every action there is an equal and opposite reaction. What this means to us is that if we emit a thousand pounds of impact force with a punch and make contact with a target, there will be a thousand pounds of reaction force either coming back into the hand or passing through the target if it cannot resist the pressure. Observe Figure 1: "A" is the sending force of "B," the weapon, which is on its way to "C," the target. "A" would be the practitioner and "B" could be a punch, for example. Following Figures 1, 2, and 3, you will observe the weapon following its course toward the target until its impact in Figure 3. At the point in Figure 1 at which the weapon has just left the chamber position, the inertial resistance puts a drain on the speed of the weapon because the weapon was not moving before this point. By the time the weapon has reached the position in Figure 2, the speed

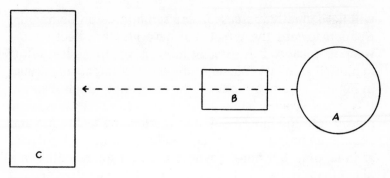

Figure 1

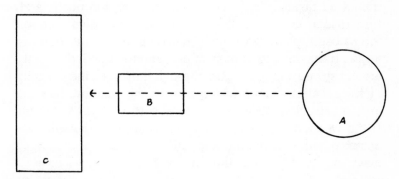

Figure 2

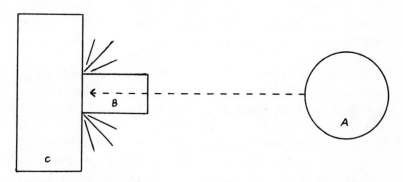

Figure 3

will have greatly increased. The same force propelling the weapon toward the target will have greater effect on the weapon because it is already moving, requiring less effort to move it along its course. At the point of impact illustrated in Figure 3, the weapon will have reached its greatest speed. It will have steadily increased in velocity from the effort being placed into the movement, and the locking technique and snapping motion of the punch will also increase the speed at this point, but here is where reaction forces come into play. Up until the point of impact, most of the forces against the weapon have been positive and propelling it in the same direction. Upon impact, however, the weapon will encounter increased negative reaction force resisting the positive effort. It is at this point that positive and negative reaction forces begin passing through the weapon and through the target. If the density of the weapon and the applied velocity are not strong enough to pass through the target, the majority of the reaction forces will return to the weapon, less the amount that the target is able to absorb without breaking. If the weapon passes through the target, the opposite will occur. Whether or not the weapon passes through the target, however, a percentage of the reaction forces will pass through the weapon. When you are conditioning your weapon for breaking, you are first training it to increase its strength and density to be able to pass through the target without damage to the weapon. You are also training it to resist and withstand the negative reaction forces that will always be present in breaking. The more easily the weapon overcomes the target, the lesser the percentage of negative reaction force. Look at Figure 4, which shows the target being contacted by the weapon. The large black arrows marked positive and negative in circles at their tips denote the force of the weapon (positive), and the resistance force of the target (negative). When these two forces meet, the reactions denoted by the thin arrows and marked with the hexagons at their tips occur. The negative reaction force returns to the weapon; the positive reaction force continues through the target. If the density of the target and the weapon are the same, and the

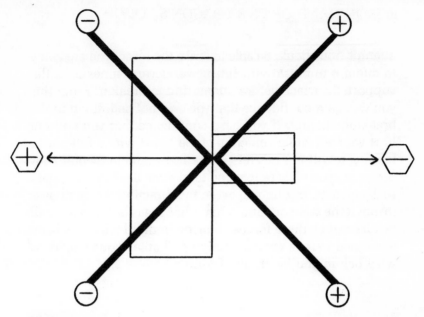

Figure 4

speed applied to the weapon is not sufficient to cause the target to break, both the target and the weapon will absorb an equal amount of reaction force. Two objects of equal density colliding will evenly share the "equal and opposite reaction." When speed is applied to the weapon, however, in an amount that will cause it to overcome the density of the target, and thereby breaking it, the greater portion of the reaction from the contact is expelled in positive force. This is, of course, theoretical and subject to variables according to Pyrrhonian standards, but experience has dictated that much greater pain, if any at all, will be felt from an unsuccessful breaking attempt than from a successful one.

What all this teaches is that a full-speed blow should always be applied in breaking attempts. Where there is a lack of confidence, hesitation at the last moment may cause you to pull your strike or slow it down at impact. Just as an improperly delivered or focused blow can cause damage to the weapon, a blow that is pulled at the last moment for the lack of confidence can also cause damage, or at least an undue amount of pain. File the illustration in Figure 4 in the back of your mind to refer to when you make your first breaking attempt. You should be able to strike the object you are going to attempt to break with full power several times on a flat supported surface before attempting to break it. From this you will gain confidence that you will not be injured in the breaking attempt. If you have confidence that you will not hurt yourself when you contact the target with a full-power blow, you will not hesitate at the last moment or pull your power or speed. These reaction forces will be discussed again in Chapter Four with respect to the direction they will pass through the weapon, and what other areas of the body will be affected by these forces. Bearing in mind what has been discussed here, a careful study of Chapter Four would be wise before you begin any training.

Chapter 2

𒀭𒀭𒀭𒀭𒀭𒀭𒀭𒀭𒀭𒀭𒀭𒀭𒀭𒀭𒀭𒀭𒀭

Anatomical Weapons of the Hand

The four most crucial weapons of the hand are the punch, backhand, suto, and palm, and it is these four weapons that will be studied in this chapter. These four strokes provide an array of striking angles at both long and short distances, and are the most devastating in terms of impact force. These are the strikes that are most likely to be used in a combative situation. Unless you have trained yourself specifically to respond with other hand strikes, it will be one of these that you will use in a reflex response, be it offense or defense.

PUNCH AND BACKHAND

Figure 5 is an overhead view of the skeletal structure of the left hand. The middle and index finger are detached, and the area enclosed by the oblong box is the area that makes the actual contact when using a straight punch or a backhand strike. They are the tips of the bones of the top of the hand. When the fist is formed, the fingers are rolled downward, exposing the area. It is this area that makes the contact, and this area that must be strengthened. Figure 6 is a head-on view of the fist with the proper area of contact noted (see also Figure 7). Form your hand into a fist and observe that

11

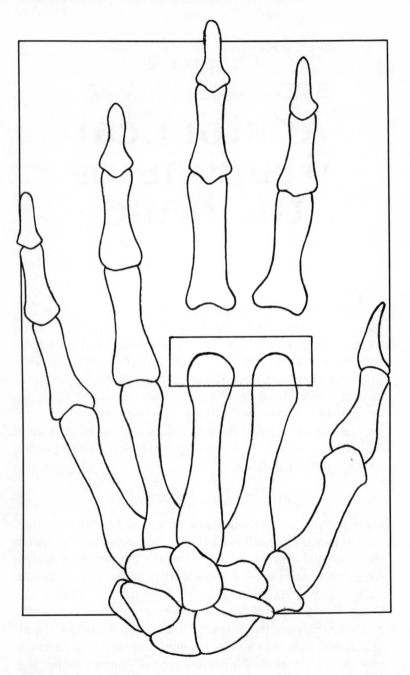

Figure 5

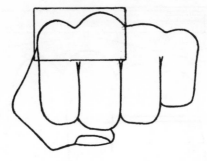

Figure 6

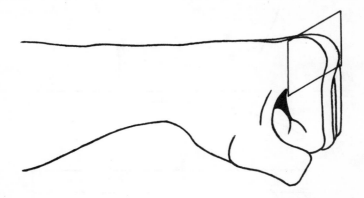

Figure 7

when this is held in a normal alignment with the forearm, only the middle knuckle would make contact with a target, along with the corresponding finger. Proper alignment will call for two adjustments. Looking back at Figure 7, note that the top of the hand is held level with the top of the forearm. If you laid it against a wall, the forearm, wrist, and fist would all be touching the wall simultaneously. This position gives the bones of the hand a perfect structural alignment with the bones of the forearm, and thus alleviates the greatest possible amount of give at the wrist joint, protecting it from sprain and maximizing resistance to negative impact force. The second adjustment that must be made is to rotate the fist slightly to the outside to allow the first and second

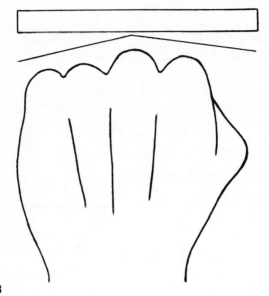

Figure 8

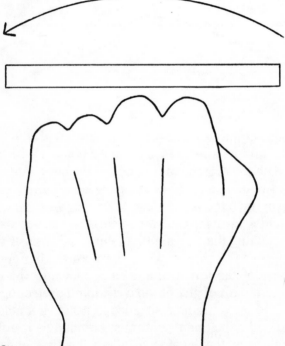

Figure 9

knuckle to strike the target surface simultaneously. Figure 8 demonstrates how the middle knuckle protrudes further than the others, requiring the rotation noted in Figure 9. Rotate the hand only as much as is necessary to compensate for the protrusion and produce a surface that will allow the first and second knuckles to contact the target together. When making this rotation, do not allow the first adjustment to be affected either upward or downward. Proper alignment is crucial to maximize power and safety to the joints.

The head-on view of the fist in Figure 10 has crossed lines at the precise area of the knuckles where the punch should be focused. Figure 10 depicts the horizontal position of the punch, but the same area is used when applying the punch

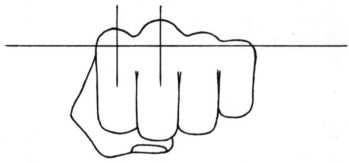

Figure 10

vertically as illustrated in Figure 11. The adjustments made at the wrist in rotating the fist to the outside and aligning the bones of the hand with the bones of the forearm are inviolable and are to be maintained in the vertical punch as well as the horizontal. A vertical punch on a target as illustrated in Figure 12 must also use only the first two knuckles. When you begin training on the practice blocks to toughen the knuckles for breaking, refer back to these illustrations as often as necessary. This alignment is a key element of power in the punch.

The backhand strike utilizes the same general area as the straight punch, but, as Figure 13 illustrates, it is the area closer to the top of the hand on the knuckles that is used

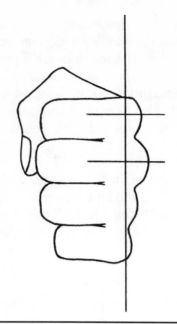

Figure 11

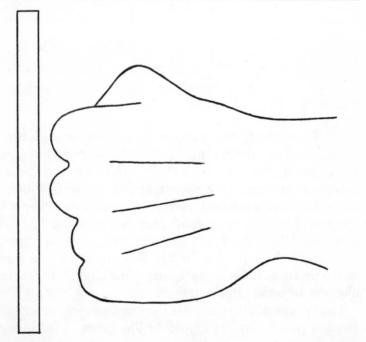

Figure 12

Figure 13

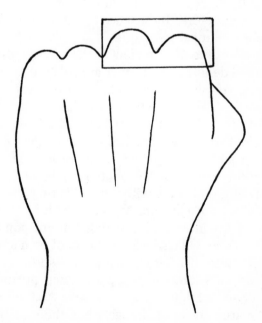

Figure 14

in this strike; therefore, the hand must be tilted at the wrist to properly form the weapon. Figure 14 denotes the proper area. Because the punch and the backhand strikes are using the same general areas, they should be trained in succession.

SUTO

The suto strike is the most versatile, most easily applied, and certainly the most devastating hand weapon on the human body. It is also the most durable and will be ready for breaking long before the other weapons of the hand. It can be applied horizontally palm-up and palm-down, vertically downward, and at an angle in a downstroke. In its full open form, it can draw power from the heel of the supporting leg and knee, the hip and shoulder, the elbow, and from centrifugal force all at the same time. Furthermore, it does not have a limited range of penetration like the punch does. Penetration can range from four inches to four feet according to the stroke used. By making a mistake, however, you can permanently damage the communicating areas of the hand very easily; therefore, the strictest attention must be paid to the proper area of this weapon.

Figure 15 is a palm-side view of the skeletal structure of the left hand denoting the proper area of contact. Following the arrows, you will see that although the wrist is in fact a weak area, when used in the proper fashion the suto strike has a great deal of structural backup behind it by approaching the wrist from the side. The actual contact area of the suto is very small, as depicted in Figure 16. The entire side of the hand is not used. The supporting bone in the top of the hand communicating with the pinkie finger is extremely fragile and sensitive to pain. At its base as it meets the bones of the wrist it widens and is strong, but any contact above the upper arrow will cause a great deal of pain and is likely to cause fracture if used against a hard surface. Figure 16 depicts the suto hand in the palm-down position, while Figures 17 and 18 depict a vertical suto. As Figure 17 illustrates, the area does not change when the direction of the stroke changes. Here again, a tilt in the wrist is required to

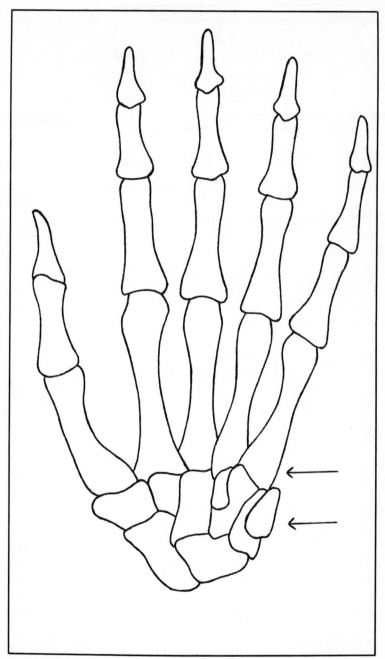

Figure 15

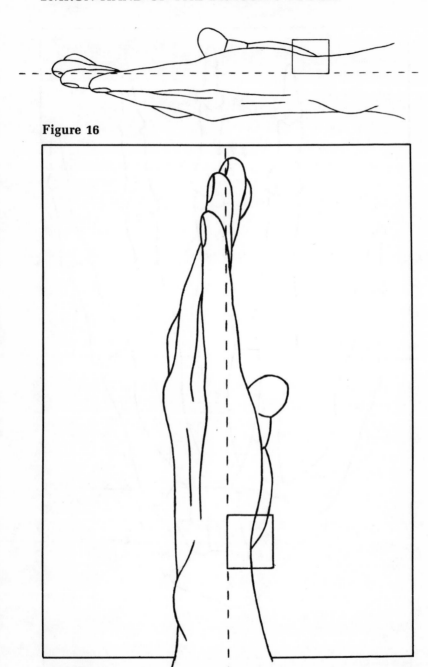

Figure 16

Figure 17

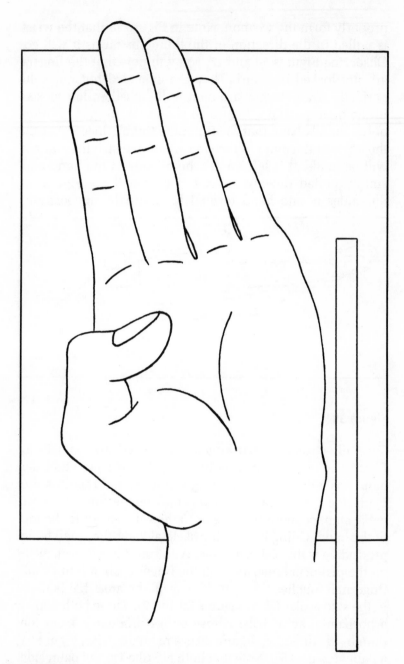

Figure 18

properly form the weapon. Note in Figure 18 that the wrist is pulled in the direction of the thumb as far as it will go. Observing Figures 16 and 17, you will note that the fingers are not locked outward. They are extended but not held perfectly straight; they are bent to lie together, but locked in the open position. Figure 18 shows the proper position of the thumb. Note that the tip of the thumb does not cross the palm of the hand to the side where the striking contact will be made. It is left on the thumb side of the hand and simply pulled downward as far as it will go. Figure 19 illustrates a suto hand formed for the palm-up position.

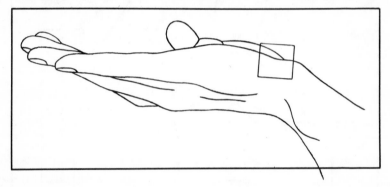

Figure 19

Carefully observe the striking area depicted, and go back to Figures 16 and 17. Looking from a side view, note that the hand has a dotted line splitting it in half, and that it is the palm-side half of the hand that is making the contact. Never make contact above this line or to the side closest to the top of the hand. Going back to the skeletal view, the small bone protruding is the pisiform bone. With your index finger, push on the pisiform bone, and roll the finger against it until the fingernail touches the skin. This is all the area that is used in the suto strike. Go to Figures 20 and 21. These both depict a horizontal suto strike whose stroke originated from the thumb-side direction. Figure 20 is a palm-up strike, Figure 21 a palm-down strike. Note that both are tilted to the palm side of the hand. Observing once again Figures 16 and 17, note

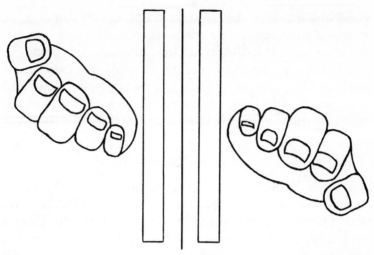

Figure 20   **Figure 21**

that the palm side of the hand is the proper striking area. If you look at either Figure 20 or 21 with the target facing your lap instead of to your right or left, you will observe the proper angle for a downward suto strike. Again, the contact is being made at the palm side of the hand. Familiarize yourself with this area; in your practice on the blocks, train your hands to form this tilt automatically and without thought.

Figure 22 depicts the hand formed for a suto in a way that would be formed by someone who has injured the pinkie

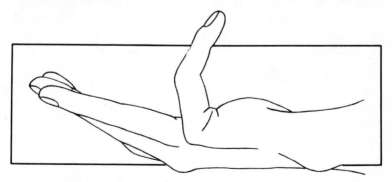

Figure 22

bone in the side of the hand from improperly forming the suto and striking a hard surface. They will be trying to flex the small muscle in the side of the hand that runs along the pinkie bone trying to protect it, and understandably so: it hurts to hit it on a hard surface. Save yourself this painful experience with the conditioning process you are about to engage in. Be sure you are hitting the proper area of the hand.

PALM

If you will look back at Figure 15 and then at Figure 23, you will notice the close proximity on the hand that is being used for the suto and the palm strike. Like the punch and backhand therefore, the suto and palm should be trained in succession.

Referring to Figure 23, the group of bones enclosed by the box is the proper area of contact. Figure 24 shows a surface view of the right hand with the contact area noted. The entire palm area is not used, and because the area is limited in terms of contact surface, a tilt of the hand is again necessary. Observe Figure 25. The hand is rotated to the pinkie side just far enough to keep the thumb side of the hand from making contact. Figure 26 shows a head-on view of the right hand making contact with a target, illustrating the tilt at the wrist. Note that the hand and fingers are held loosely. Spread the fingers comfortably and leave the thumbs open. Do not lock the thumb down as was done in forming the suto hand.

As noted in the suto area description, this area of the hand is dense and strong. The palm strike, therefore, like the suto, will condition quickly and be ready for breaking long before the punch or backhand strikes.

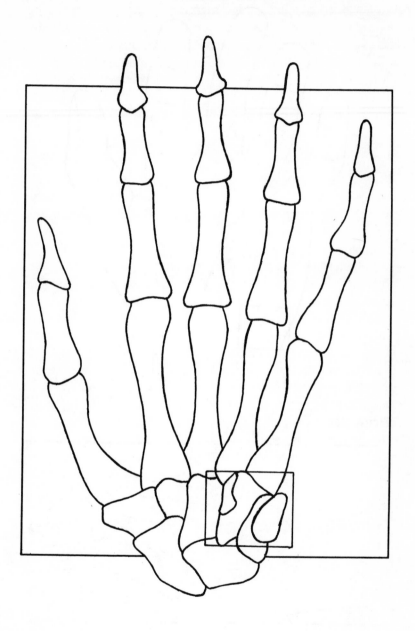

Figure 23

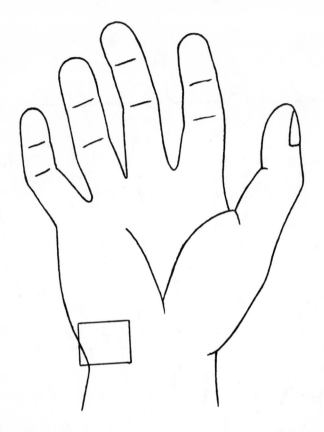

Figure 24

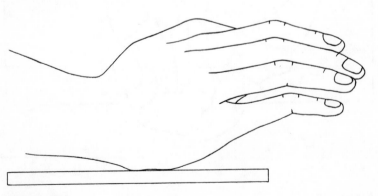

Figure 25

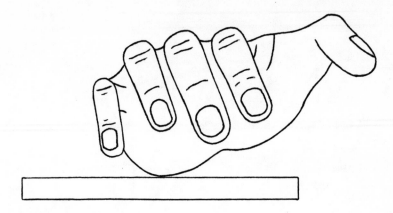

Figure 26

Chapter 3

Anatomical Weapons of the Feet

In this chapter we are going to study the three anatomical weapons of the feet that are most often used in breaking techniques. These three are the most useful in a combative situation as well. You will also find that within these three kicks you will have covered the majority of kicking contact areas applied in most styles of kung-fu and karate in the various other kicks.

Just as angles and concentration points were important factors in applying the weapons of the hand, those same factors are of equal importance here. There are fragile areas on the foot very close to the areas that you will be developing for breaking, so as in the study of hand weapons, care should be taken in locating the areas on your own body and using them properly and accurately.

FRONT KICK

Figure 27 is a skeletal illustration of the right foot. There is a dotted line passing through the illustration, and there is a black arrow showing an angle of approximately twelve degrees. The dotted line illustrates the ideal angle for the negative impact force to pass through the foot. The black arrow illustrates the most common direction that this

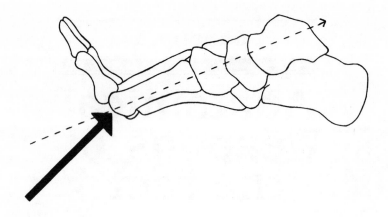

Figure 27

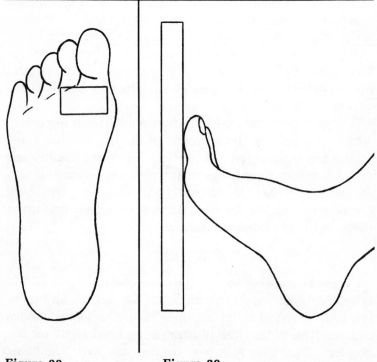

Figure 28   **Figure 29**

reaction force will pass through the foot. Figure 28 shows the precise area of contact on a target when using the front kick. In Figure 29, the right foot is shown against a target as it will typically make the contact. Because the knee is the fulcrum point of the kick, where the knee is (in relation to the height of the target) will determine exactly how much the toes are required to bend backward. The toes must be pulled back as far as they will go as the kick is delivered. At the angle depicted by Figure 29, the toes will be safe from injury on contact with the target regardless of its strength. This target is at a ninety-degree angle with the floor. In Figure 30, the target is parallel with the floor as it would be in practicing an overhead break with the front kick. The toes are bent back considerably further, but this is not the result of a controlled effort. If you were breaking an overhead object with the front kick, the toes would probably contact the target first and be pushed out of the way as the kick continued toward the target and finally made full contact. At times a mild sprain will occur when the toes are forced back this

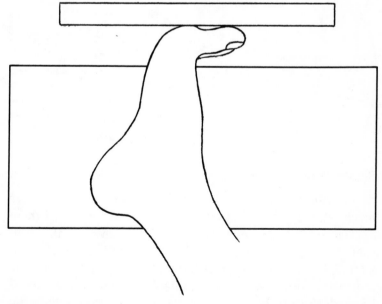

Figure 30

far, but in time the ligaments will stretch, allowing the toes to bend back this far without strain. If you have trouble getting your toes back, it would be wise to stretch them back with your hands or by kneeling on the floor with your toes bent and the ball of the foot resting on the floor. Gently apply pressure to the toes to loosen the joints. If you thrust a front kick out and hit a firm target with your toes not pulled back, they would more than likely be broken. Keep your toes pulled back at all times when delivering this kick.

HOOK KICK

A hook kick applied in sparring is often executed by making a slapping-type contact with the ball end of the foot or with the entire bottom of the foot landing flush. The hook kick as applied in a combative situation is the same type that will be studied here as a breaking weapon. Observe Figure 31, a skeletal illustration of the right foot with two areas noted. The area pointed to by the black arrow is the proper area of contact for the hook kick. The area sectioned off by the

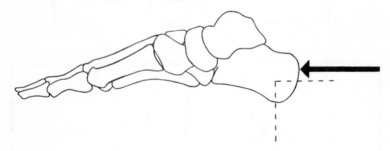

Figure 31

dotted ninety-degree angle is the area that you will never forget striking a hard target with if you are unfortunate enough to make the mistake. Figure 32 shows the direction that the negative reaction force will pass through the foot as noted by the dotted line. Precisely where the dotted line enters the foot is where the contact with the target should be made. Figure 33 is a rear-angle view of the foot, with the exact area of contact depicted by cross lines. In Figure 34

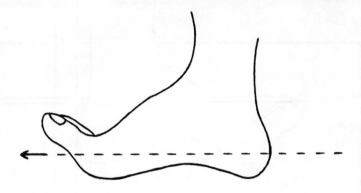

Figure 32

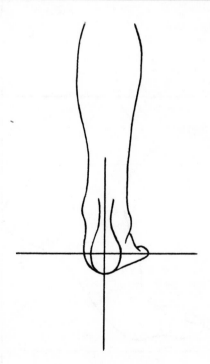

Figure 33

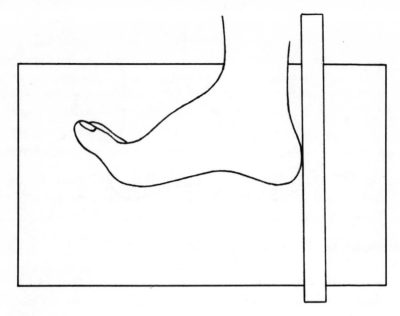

Figure 34

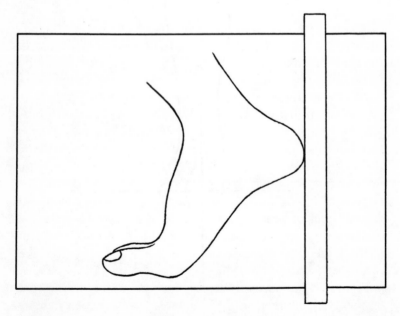

Figure 35

the foot is shown striking a target at the proper angle. The very back of the heel at its highest point is the contact area. Look now at Figure 35. This is an improperly executed hook kick. It is making contact with the point of the heel. The first time you hit a target with your heel at this angle will most likely be the last, because you will remember that pain for a long time. The point of the heel is extremely sensitive to contact with hard objects. Go back to Figure 31 and observe once again the area sectioned off by the dotted line. Do not make contact with this area on any hard object. Any anatomical targets below the bony part of the head are soft enough to strike with the point of the heel, excluding joints, but contact to the head, knees, elbows, hip girdle, or any other hard object will cause extreme pain to the heel. It is best to break any habit of using the point of the heel in this kick. Study this weapon carefully before beginning any training on practice blocks. Injury to this area could take as long as six months to heal.

SIDE KICK

Because the side kick applies an area very close to the area used in the hook kick, and specifically the danger area of the heel, look back now again at Figure 31. Pay close attention to the area sectioned off by the ninety-degree dotted lines. Look now at Figure 36. The area within the dotted lines here is your weapon area. The most critical area of danger in the side kick is that area pointed to by the black arrow. Locate this area on your foot. The point of this bone runs right along the edge of the foot that you will be training and applying in breaking. You must avoid hitting this area at all costs. This bone will chip or break if it strikes a hard object, and without a great deal of pressure. Look now at Figure 37. Note the contact area shown as being the final edge on the heel end of the foot. The dotted arrow depicts the direction that the negative reaction force will pass through the foot. Look now at Figure 38. Note that there is a small portion of the bottom of the heel being used in the kick. This area is heavily protected and misses the bottom area of the heel bone. Figure

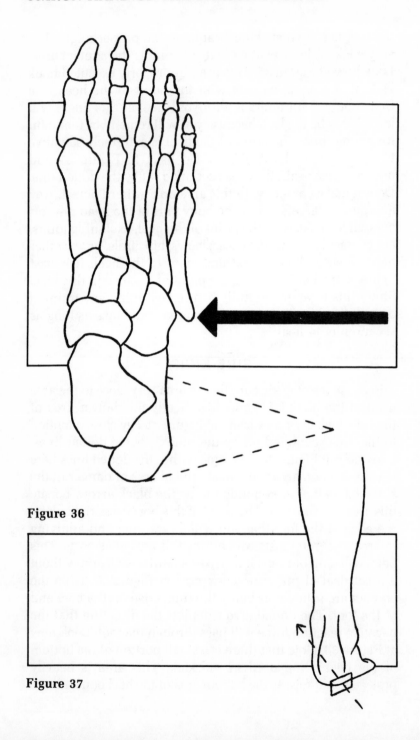

Figure 36

Figure 37

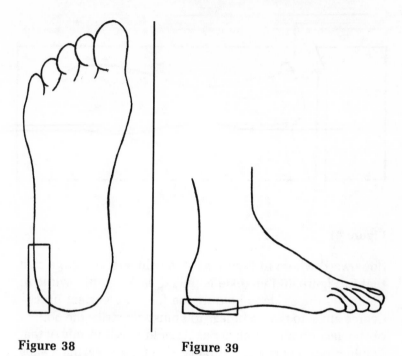

Figure 38   **Figure 39**

39 shows the outer view of the right foot with the contact area for the side kick enclosed. Look closely now at Figures 40 and 41. Figure 40 illustrates a properly executed side kick making contact with a target, while Figure 41 shows the kick landing improperly. Note in Figure 40 that the ankle is bent

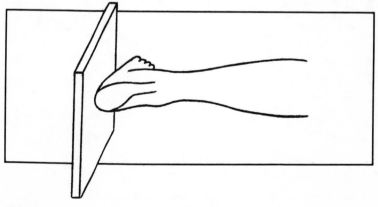

Figure 40

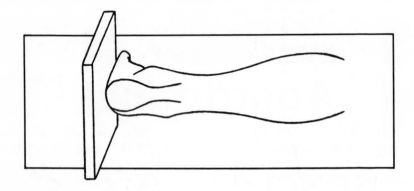

Figure 41

downward where in Figure 41 it is held straight. Note also that in Figure 40 the ankle is pulled back slightly, while in Figure 41 the ankle is holding the foot at a perfect ninety-degree angle to the lower leg. You must not strike the bottom of the heel on a hard object as it could result in injury that would require corrective surgery. If you are wearing a shoe while fighting, you can use the bottom of the heel. Barefoot application of the side kick will require proper positioning as depicted in Figure 40.

Chapter 4

Anatomical Weapons and Reaction Areas

In Chapter One we discussed positive and negative impact forces, illustrating how they interact with the weapon and with the target. We will go one step further here. We will show how negative impact force continues passing from the point of impact through the weapon until it has been absorbed. This shock in a punch, for example, can be felt in the shoulder, abdomen, and even in the heel of the rear leg, according to how great the returning force is. As this returning force passes through the weapon, it will be seeking a weak area in the arm or leg from which to escape, and will either find such an area or continue traveling through the body until it is diminished through absorption. The term *escape* as intended here does not mean to harmlessly pass away; it means that the shock would be spent in consuming a bone or a joint. It is highly unlikely that a bone in the arm or leg would crack or break under this pressure, being that the joints are weaker. Therefore, Chapter Four will include a study of the major joints that will be affected by the shock.

Figure 42 is an illustration of an extended punch. When this punch contacts its target, the first reaction is felt in the weapon itself. Following the initial shock, however, the reac-

39

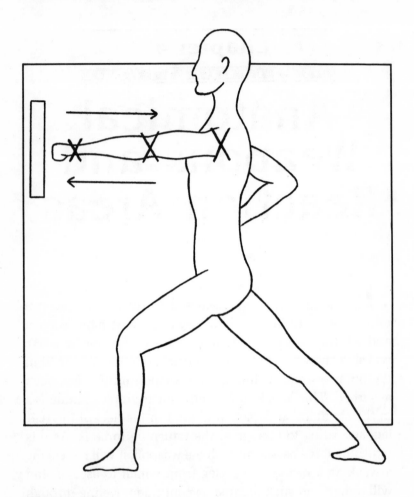

Figure 42

tion force will continue to travel through the weapon into
the wrist, the elbow, and into the shoulder. For the straight-
line punch, these three areas (marked by an X) are the major
weak areas that will be affected by the returning force.

Figure 43 is an illustration of an extended backhand strike.
Note the direction of the arrows. Because the body is not
behind the weapon, the majority of the returning force is
spent passing through the weapon itself. There is shock to
the wrist but, as a rule, there will be no shock felt in other

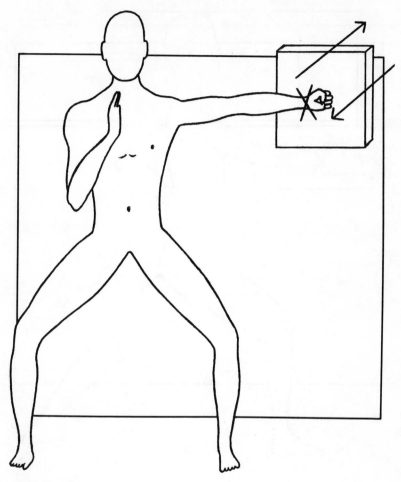

Figure 43

areas of the body unless the strike has been improperly
delivered.

Observe now Figures 44 and 45. Figure 44 is a vertical suto,
and 45 is a vertical palm. The final six inches of these two
strikes are very similar, and the extended arm in Figure 45
would not be an incorrect position for the suto, nor would
the bent arm in Figure 44 be incorrect in applying the palm.
The positioning of the elbow in these two strikes structurally
controls the depth of the strokes. For both the vertical suto

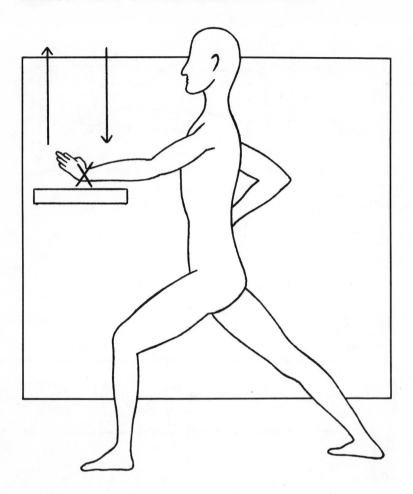

Figure 44

and the vertical palm, therefore, a bent arm application would confine the shock to the wrist, whereas the extended arm application would allow the shock to pass on into the elbow. The X indicates the affected areas.

Figure 46 illustrates a front kick in the fully opened position. The arrows indicate the typical path for the positive and negative reaction forces to travel. The most affected areas for this stroke are again noted by the X. The kick illustrated is at hip level. When the front kick is used above the waist,

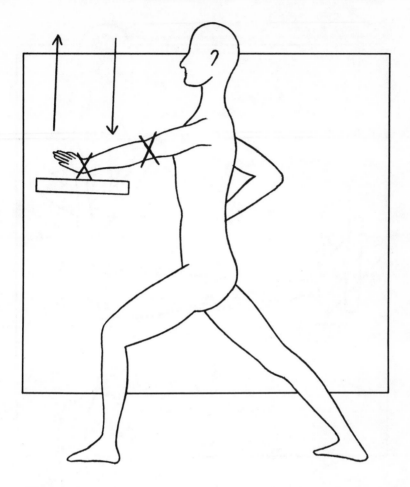

Figure 45

the shock will also pass through the hip. If you look back now at Figure 42, taking notice of the arrows denoting the positive and negative impact forces, and then look at the arrows in Figure 46 comparing the number of joints involved in the reaction process, you will see that the more solid the backup structure of the stroke is, the greater the amount and distance of the shock to the body.

Figure 47 illustrates an extended hook kick. The shock for this movement will be restricted to the ankle and to the knee

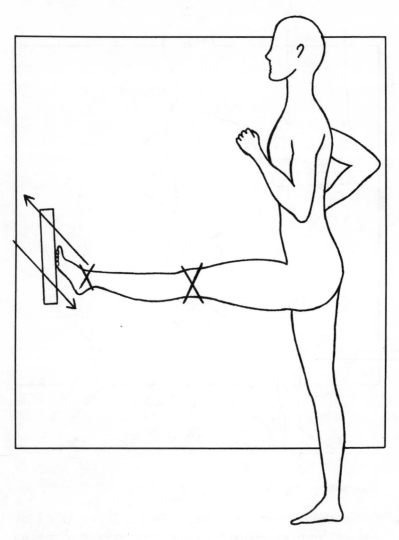

Figure 46

as indicated by the X markings.

In Figure 48 the side kick is illustrated with the major joints receiving a reaction to the negative impact force denoted. Once again, go back to Figure 42 and observe that illustration, comparing it to this one. Both the side kick and the straight-line punch are thrusts involving strokes of limited penetra-

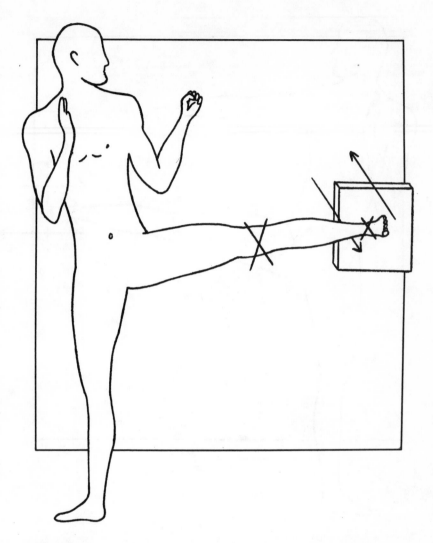

Figure 47

tion. At their extended points, both have the body structure behind them. The other five strokes illustrated here draw power from centrifugal force involving an arc in the movement. At their extended points, the body is *not* behind the weapon. What is noteworthy to remember here is that the straight-line punch and the side kick, both being thrust

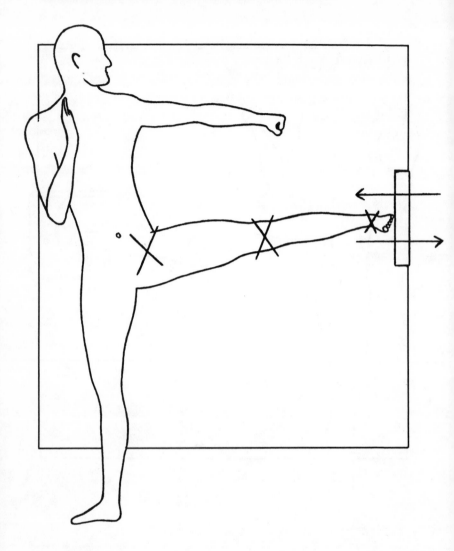

Figure 48

movements and having the body structure behind them, are
in fact limited as far as depth and penetration, but they are
more solid than the other five and are able to emit a force
that is less likely to be resisted by a target, because more
muscle and body weight are behind both. These two strokes,
because they are shorter, will also be quicker in terms of the

time it takes for the weapon to leave the body's chamber position and reach its target. The centrifugal force blows will have amassed greater speed by the time they contact the target, but because they involve a longer stroke, the time it takes for the blow to reach the target will also be greater.

STRENGTHENING REACTION AREAS

We just learned that the reaction to negative impact force as discussed in Chapter One will go beyond the anatomical weapon and reach into other areas of the body. Now we will study how to strengthen these areas with rather simple but important exercises. These exercises will be numbered, and in the chapter giving the training process they will be referred to and be an integral portion of the routine.

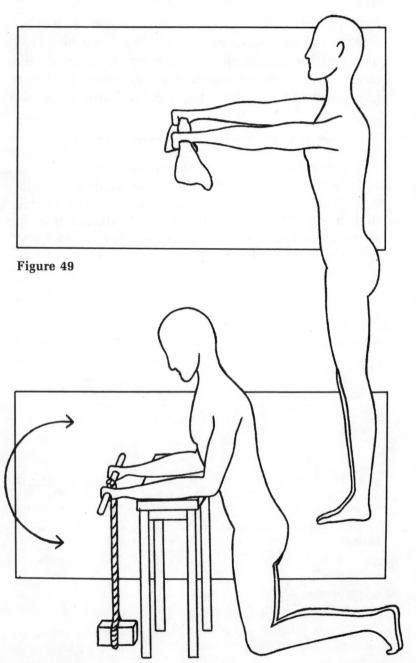

Figure 49

Figure 50

Exercise #1

In Figure 49, a towel is being held at arm's length. By squeezing the towel as hard as you can and then releasing it, you are exercising the muscles that control the hand, fingers, and wrist. A strong forearm will give power to the wrist and hands, strengthening both for breaking and other uses as well.

Exercises #2 and #3

In Figure 50, a brick is tied to a stick for resistance, and the wrists are to follow the arc as depicted by the arrow. Relax the wrists, allowing them to bend downward as far as they will go, then pull them upward as far as they will go. This exercise will further strengthen the wrists and forearms. The palm-down position depicted in Figure 50 is exercise #2. To perform exercise #3, reverse the grip on the stick, holding the palms facing upward with the tops of the forearms resting on the table. Follow the same arc of the movement. Exercise #2 strengthens the wrist and top of the forearm, while exercise #3 strengthens the inside of the forearm and the wrist.

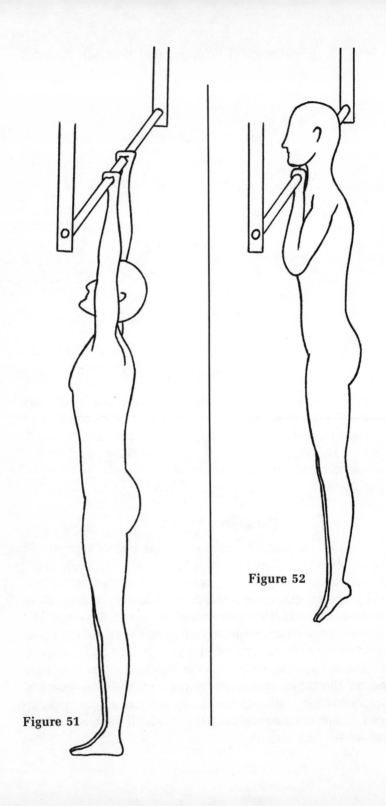

Figure 51

Figure 52

Exercises #4 and #5

The illustrations in Figures 51 and 52 depict the positions for the fourth and fifth exercises. Exercise #4 is the pull-up, executed by pulling the chin up to the bar, palms facing away from the body. To position yourself for exercise #5, simply grip the bar with the palms facing you instead of away from you, again pulling your body up until the chin reaches the bar. Exercise #4 strengthens the lats, shoulder blades, and sides of the shoulder caps. Exercise #5 works essentially the same areas but includes the biceps as well.

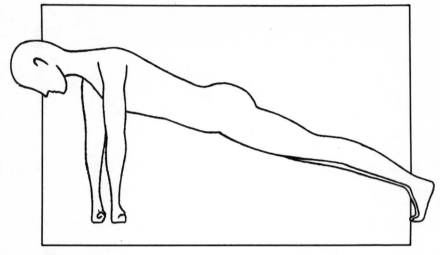

Figure 53

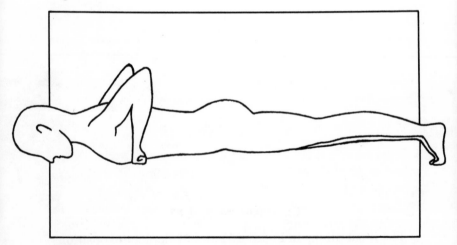

Figure 54

Exercise #6

Depicted by Figures 53 and 54, the push-up strengthens a variety of muscles in the upper body. When performed on a closed fist as illustrated here instead of on the palms, the wrist is also strengthened. The elbows should be held close to the body during the entire exercise.

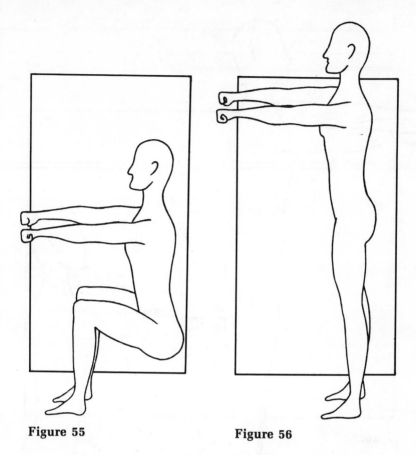

Figure 55   **Figure 56**

Exercises #7 and #8

Here we begin working the muscles of the lower body. In exercise #7, the feet will be positioned under the shoulders as depicted by Figure 55. Exercise #8 requires a wider stance, at least six inches beyond the span of the shoulders. To perform the movement, squat at the knee joint just far enough to break the parallel plane between the upper leg and the floor (Figure 56), and return to the standing position. It is important to break the parallel plane to bring the buttocks thoroughly into play in the movement. These two exercises are going to strengthen the quadriceps, femoral biceps, and buttocks, all of which will increase the power output of your kicks and strengthen the reaction areas affected by negative impact force. If necessary, use a chair or other object to maintain your balance during the exercise.

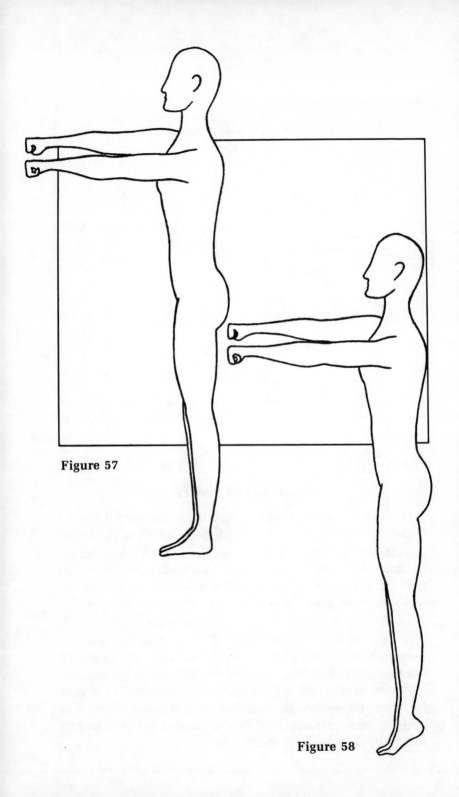

Figure 57

Figure 58

Exercise #9

In Figures 57 and 58, the simple exercise illustrated will greatly strengthen the calf muscles, which play an important role in ankle strength and movement. With the feet held together, simply extend the ankles downward, raising the body up and on the balls of the feet. Again, a chair or wall may be used to maintain balance.

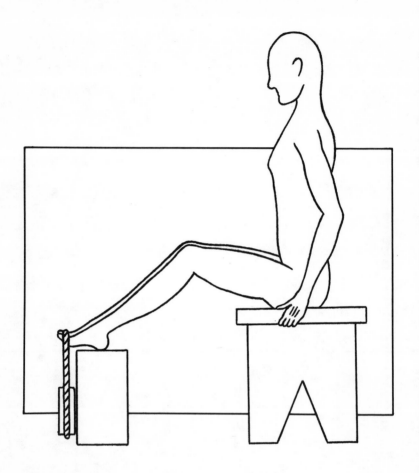

Figure 59

Exercise #10

Figures 59 and 60 illustrate the final exercise. A brick, used here for resistance, is tied to a rope and held in the crook of the toes. Extend the ankles forward as far as they will go, then draw them upward as far as they will go. The tiny muscles in the foot and around the ankle, and the muscles around the shin bone are being worked in this movement. As the ankle will receive a shock in all kicking techniques,

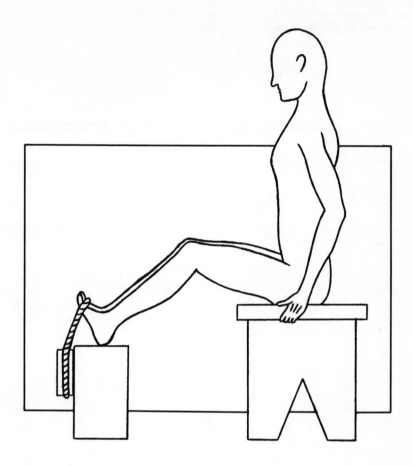

Figure 60

it is important to strengthen the area as much as possible.

The number of sets and repetitions for each of these exercises will be given in the chapter covering the training process. Perform these exercises slowly and always use the maximum range of movement of each. It is as important to have your muscular power up to par in breaking as it is to have the contact areas conditioned. Do not shortcut on this area of training.

Chapter 5

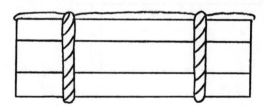

Construction of Training Blocks

We have thus far discussed positive and negative reaction forces, the anatomy of hand and foot weapons, where reaction forces will be felt in the body, and how to strengthen the respective areas. Having come this far, we will now discuss training blocks and how they may be constructed.

Figure 61 is a typical example of a hand-held practice block. It can be held on the floor with one hand and struck

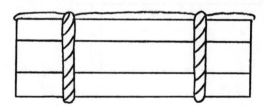

Figure 61

with the other, or held vertically by a training partner. This training block is composed of two pieces of rope approximately twenty-four inches long, a piece of burlap-backed carpet about six by twelve inches, two one-inch boards measuring six by twelve inches, and a piece of foam rubber also measuring six by twelve inches. Figure 62 is an exploded diagram of the hand-held training block. At the very top is

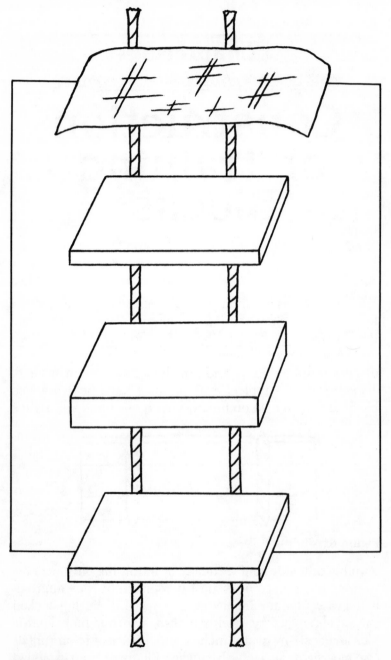

Figure 62

a piece of burlap-backed carpet faced with the burlap side outward. Burlap is a very coarse material and will be hard on the skin, causing tiny cuts which will begin building a surface callous. Under the section of carpet is a six-by-twelve board to make the striking surface rigid. Under that board is a piece of foam rubber followed by another board, all measuring the same, six by twelve. The foam between the two boards allows the striking block to give against the pressure of the blows. In time, as the hands and feet grow used to the block and can be hit at full power, the density of the target can be increased by removing the foam and inserting a less pressure-absorbing material between the boards, such as three or four layers of terry cloth or some similar type of material. Once the materials are cut and ready to put together, it is best to pile them on the floor in their proper order and have someone stand on top of the pile while it is being tied. This will allow a firm binding of the ropes around the loose materials, reducing the frequency of tightening the ropes which will be needed periodically. To again increase the density of the target, simply remove the terry cloth one layer at a time until you are hitting the block with no pressure-absorbing material between the boards. Never make such an adjustment unless you are capable of hitting the block full power without pain.

Figure 63 depicts a wall-mounted striking block with the same structural features as the hand-held type. This block measures twelve by twelve inches. Figure 64 is an exploded diagram of the wall-mounted unit. To the far left is the burlap back carpet, again with the burlap faced to the striking area. A board follows, followed by a piece of foam rubber. The structure mounted to the wall should be preconstructed as one solid unit and should be put together with glue and screws. Figure 65 is a rear view of the solid section of the unit. None of these parts are to be moveable; this should be one solid section. The three-piece rear face allows the ropes to pass freely behind the unit after it is mounted to avoid having to take it down to change the burlap surface or density.

Figure 66 illustrates a floor block, which is nothing more

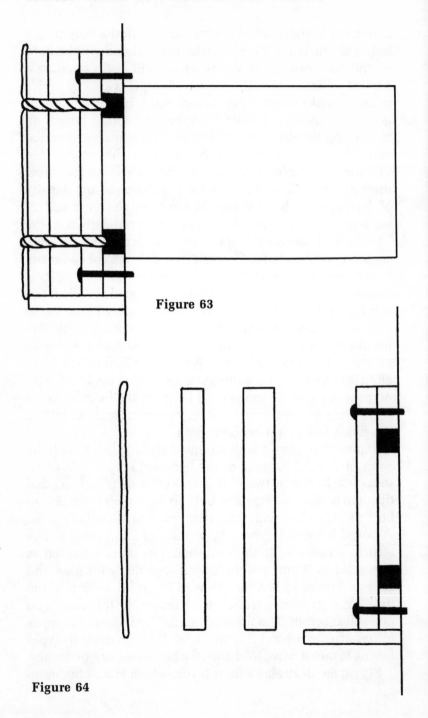

Figure 63

Figure 64

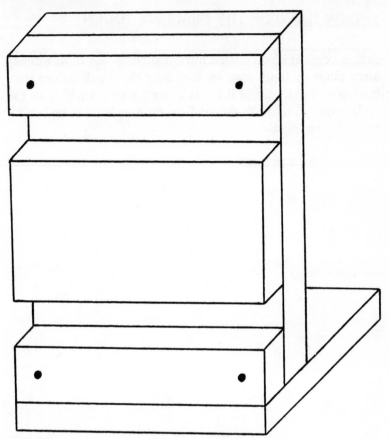

Figure 65

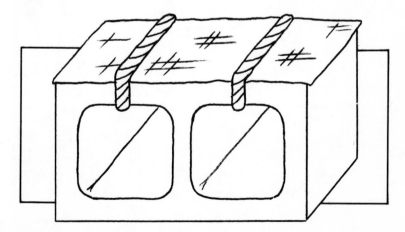

Figure 66

than a cement block with a burlap surface tied to it. Either terry cloth or foam may be laid over the block before the burlap is tied to it, but if foam is used a board will have to be laid over it to make the surface rigid enough to be beneficial for training.

Chapter 6

The Training Process

We have now been through the necessary prerequisite studies to prepare you for the training process. If there is any doubt in your mind at this point about the contact areas of the anatomical weapons, stop now and go back over the material until you are satisfied that you have a full understanding of your hand and foot weapons. Every mistake you make from this point forward will be a costly one.

At this stage you will have to begin a self-study, joining fact and philosophy with trial-and-error experience. Be cautious and deliberate in your efforts to make gains in your training without injury. Combine the teaching here with that self-study; you must become your own instructor.

PUNCH

In the illustration in Figure 67, you are standing in front of the wall-mounted unit. Both hands are in the chamber position and you are in a forward stance. Measure the depth of your punch so that when it is extended you will have approximately one inch of penetration into the target. Adjust your distance from the target accordingly. When you send your punch forward, you should be using half of your power

65

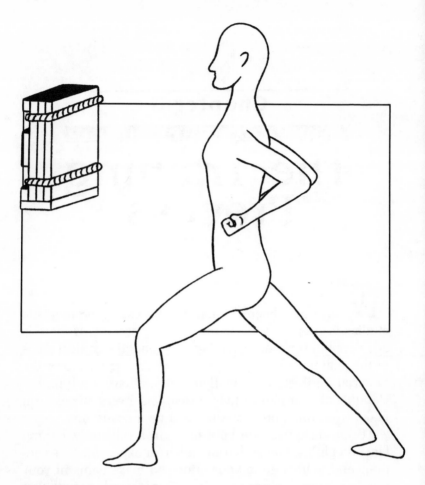

Figure 67

and half of your speed. It is important not to pull your punches; rather, extend them to the fully open position. If the target is too hard to do this, put a layer of towel under the burlap. It is better to use half power and half speed on a softer target than to use a lesser punching capacity on a hard target. Keep in mind that you are conditioning bones, muscles, and joints along with your weapon surfaces. Get in the habit of using your strikes at their proper range and extension. The technique of your strikes is of equal importance to the long-term ability in breaking.

For the exercise in Figure 68 you will be using a ten-by-four, forty-repetition formula. Here the left punch is extended into the target. The right punch will follow, then the left, and so on for a count of twenty, which will give you a total of ten repetitions on each hand. Keep your focal points in mind and adjust the movement as necessary to strike the target with the proper area of the hand. Once you have set your stance in the proper range, do not move your feet until you have completed the set of twenty repetitions. Rapid punching is taboo. One breath should be taken in and one expelled

Figure 68

between each punch; these are single-stroke concentration punches.

After your first set of punches, get a towel and perform exercise #1 (see Chapter Four) for fifty repetitions, squeezing your hands in an alternating sequence until you have completed the fifty repetitions. After the training exercise on the towel, wait two minutes, return to the conditioning block, and repeat another set of twenty punches. Again perform exercise #1 for fifty repetitions, alternating the right hand with the left. Repeat the entire sequence four times until you have thrown a total of eighty punches on the block and completed two hundred repetitions on the towel. Keep a close watch on the knuckles as you are going through the punching sets. If a soft puffiness begins to develop on or around the knuckles, stop the training and go to the next phase of the hand-conditioning process. If this happens again on your next training day, wait two weeks before punching again. This is the result of the target being too hard, and it will be necessary to add two or three additional layers of padding under the burlap. This fluid buildup on the knuckles must not be permitted.

BACKHAND

In Figure 69 you are again set for training on the wall-mounted block. Your back and stance are parallel to the wall. Stand in a straddle stance, with your feet spread a little more than shoulder-width apart and your weight evenly distributed on your legs. Measure the distance and depth of your stroke to penetrate one inch into the target. Again, you are to use half power and half speed with full extension of the strike. Take one breath in and let one breath out between strikes. Always return the arm to the full chamber position as illustrated in Figure 69; do not allow the elbow to hang in the air. Figure 70 illustrates the left hand contacting the target. For the backhand, you will do ten repetitions on the left and then move to the opposite side of the target, resetting your stance to do the repetitions of the right hand. You are again on a ten-rep, four-set sequence, a total of forty repetitions on each hand. When you have completed ten repetitions on each hand, perform exercise #2 for twenty repetitions. Wait two minutes and repeat the sequence using exercise #2. Following your third and fourth sets of backhand strikes, perform exercise #3 instead of exercise #2. The striking

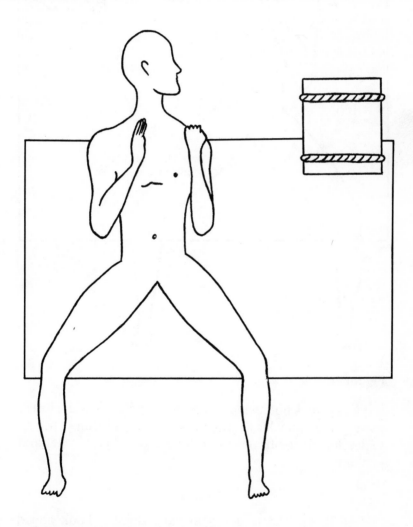

Figure 69

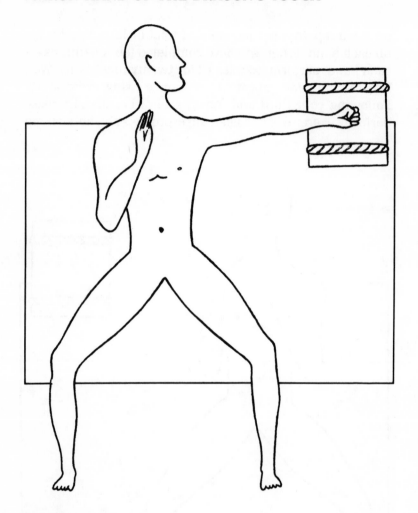

Figure 70

sequence does not change, only the exercise. Again, closely observe the knuckles during these sets. If a puffiness begins to develop, discontinue the training and go to the next hand position.

SUTO

Here the stroke is going to vary slightly. Look ahead to Chapter Seven and observe Figure 89, comparing it to

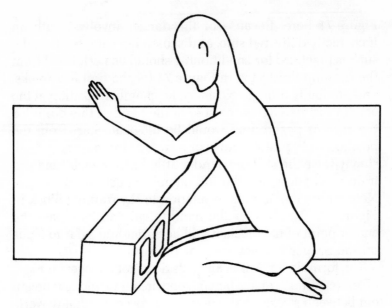

Figure 71

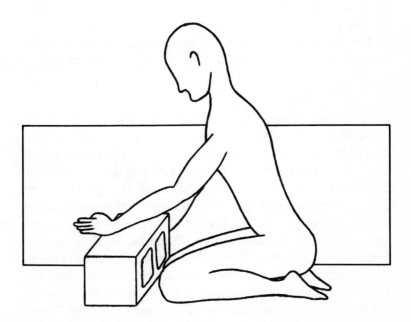

Figure 72

Figure 71 here. Because of the danger involved with an incorrectly delivered suto, as discussed in Chapter Two, the suto as practiced for conditioning should be performed from the position illustrated in Figure 71 for the first few weeks, and gradually brought closer to the chamber position at the ear. To risk damaging the side of the hand at this point for the sake of positioning would be illogical. Start from the position in Figure 71 and over a two- or three-week period, slowly raise the striking hand a little further each time you train until you reach the full chamber position at the ear. Note where the hand is in relation to the training block in Figure 72. By allowing the hand to substantially pass the center point of the block, it will be easier and safer to focus on the proper contact area for the suto.

The formula for strikes and sets does not change: four sets of ten repetitions on each hand, one breath in and one breath out between strokes, half power, half speed, gradually working your starting point in the suto up to the full chamber position. After your first and second sets, perform exercise #4. After the third and fourth sets, perform exercise #5. Sets of five to eight repetitions on both exercises will be sufficient at the start, but work your way up to sets of ten.

PALM

We're going to use the same shortened form for the palm strike as was used with the suto, and, again, the contact area on the block will be advanced forward of the center point. The leg positions illustrated for practicing the suto and the palm strikes are not mandatory. Sit comfortably, but be sure you are alert and concentrating on each strike. Four sets of ten repetitions is still the formula, with one breath in and one breath out between strikes. Exercise #6 is to be performed in numbers of repetitions that require a working of the muscles, but not to the point of exhaustion. Hold the wrist rigid during this push-up. The sequence is one set of ten repetitions on each hand as illustrated by Figures 73 and 74 on the block, and one set of exercise #6. The process is to be repeated four times until you have completed forty

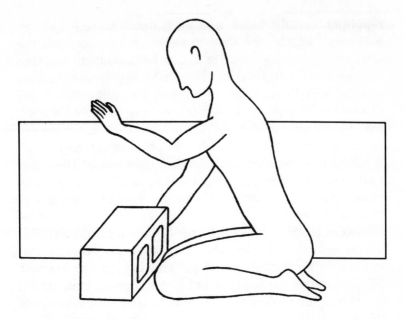

Figure 73

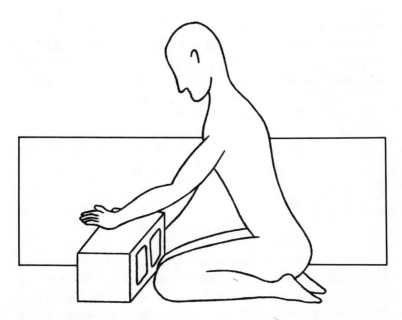

Figure 74

repetitions on the block with each hand. In your last set, and especially on the final three or four strokes, use the maximum striking force you can bear. This instruction applies to all hand strikes. Your next step in the training process will bring you some relief, but some additional discomfort as well. It is an important step in conditioning. Do not skip it.

Fill up a pot or a bucket with hot water that is large enough in which to submerge both hands simultaneously. The water should be as hot as you can stand it and should be heavily salted. Submerge your hands in the water for about five minutes, or until the water no longer feels hot to your hands. Take your hands out of the water, but do not dry them. Put a coating of dry salt directly on the areas you have trained against the block and leave it on. The salt is going to cause the skin to thicken, and the hot water is going to help heal the surface and internal areas of your weapons. Wait about one minute, add a little hot water to the bucket to compensate for the heat loss over the time that has passed since you removed your hands from the water, and submerge your salted hands back into the bucket.

Here is where you are going to find out how badly you want your hands conditioned, because after salting the striking areas, they're going to be extremely sensitive. When you submerge your hands in the water this time it's going to sting, and the sting is going to be intense for the first thirty seconds. Leave your hands submerged until the stinging stops, then remove them. Without drying your hands, salt them one more time and let them dry on their own. When your hands are dry, brush the salt off. You have finished your first day of training.

FRONT KICK

Kicks are trained separately from hand techniques, and this is day two of your training. Observe Figure 75. You are using a forward stance again, but set at a range for a front kick this time. As in the hand strikes, set your range so that the extended kick has approximately one inch of penetration into the target. In Figure 76 you have shifted your body weight onto the left leg, moving forward and locking the front kick into the target. Always return to the position in Figure 75 before throwing the next kick. Again, you will be using a ten-by-four, forty-repetition formula. Always inhale deeply and exhale before repeating a kick. When you have completed ten repetitions on one leg, change stances and throw ten kicks with the other leg. After you throw ten kicks with each leg, perform exercise #7. This exercise should be performed in sets of fifteen to twenty-five according to your individual strength. Exercise #7 should follow your first two sets of ten kicks, and exercise #8 should follow your second two sets of ten kicks. Finding the proper range for practice on the front kick will take time, and as you begin to tire, the penetration may vary. Concentration on the technique and maintaining rigidity in your form will help alleviate the problem of variation.

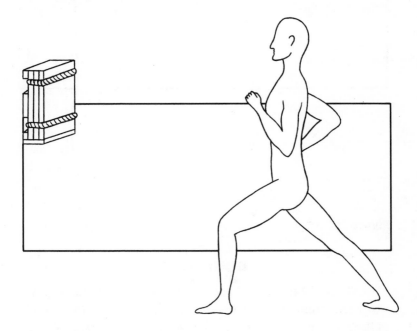

Figure 75

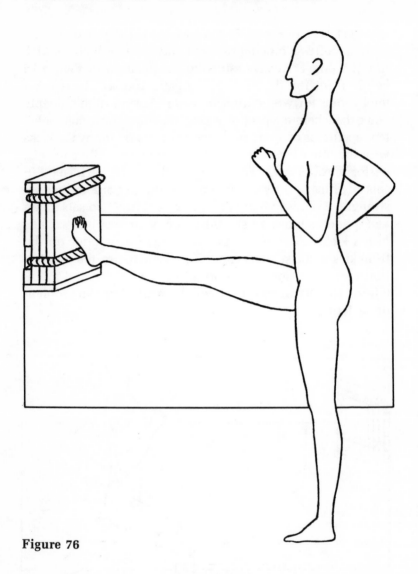

Figure 76

HOOK KICK

In Figure 77 the hook kick is depicted in its chamber position. The hook kick has two forms: the closed form, which is thrown almost like a side kick, and the wide form, which approaches its target in an arc from the chamber position shown here. The closed form is much quicker but is very

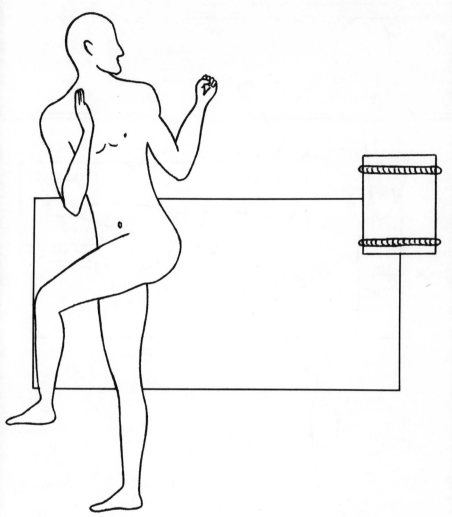

Figure 77

limited in power. The wide form is slower but its potential for power is much greater. Test your range several times before throwing the first kick of your ten-repetition set. Be sure that the extended kick lands on the proper area of the heel (Figure 78). Remember the cautions that were given in Chapter Three with regard to the point of the heel. With your range properly set, throw ten hook kicks with the left leg,

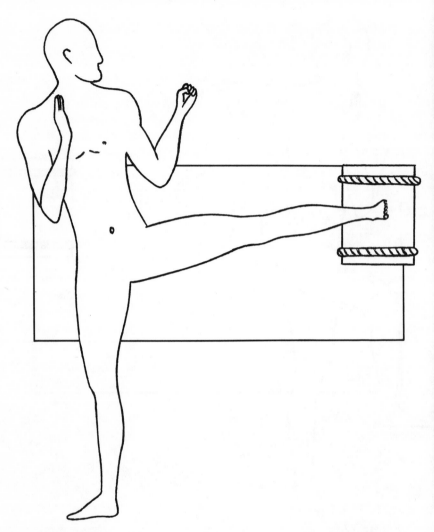

Figure 78

change stances to the opposite side of the target, and throw
ten with the right leg. It is not necessary to keep the
chambered position between kicks. Rest the foot on the floor
and chamber when you have taken your breath in and out
and are ready to throw the next kick. After you have completed ten kicks on each side, perform exercise #9 as illustrated in Figures 57 and 58 (Chapter Four). The four-set, ten-

repetition formula is also used here. The exercise will be done in sets of fifty repetitions.

SIDE KICK

The side kick will give you the greatest problems with regard to controlling the depth and resulting penetration that will be the essence of your balance. Once the side kick is locked into the fully opened position, there is no give anywhere in its structure and the negative reaction force is pushing in a straight line to the opposing hip, which will push you off balance if the kick is overpowered by the target. For this reason, you must measure your penetration and set your stance with the hip fully opened into the kick. If you measure your penetration with the leg extended but the hip not rotated into the kick, you are going to have approximately two more inches of penetration when you add your hip movement. The reaction forces have to respond to the additional penetration, which means that your kick will have to crush the target, making space for the added depth, or you will be forced backward and off balance. It will take time and practice to effectively train your side kick for breaking. In time you will develop an eye sense that will allow you to look at a target and know for which strikes you're in range. Be patient with yourself and learn from the complications you encounter.

Figure 79 shows the side kick in its chambered position. Note that the thigh is raised and held parallel to the target. The standing foot is pointed away from the target, and there should be a direct line from the heel of this foot to the exact point of contact on the target where the striking foot will land. Figure 80 illustrates the extended kick. Your sets and repetitions are again the four-by-ten, forty-repetition formula, and exercise #10 is to be performed in sets of fifteen following each set of ten right and ten left kicks. Rest the foot of the kicking leg on the floor during your breathing stops, and change the stance from right to left accordingly to train each kick. The salt-soaking procedure used for the hands should also be used on the feet.

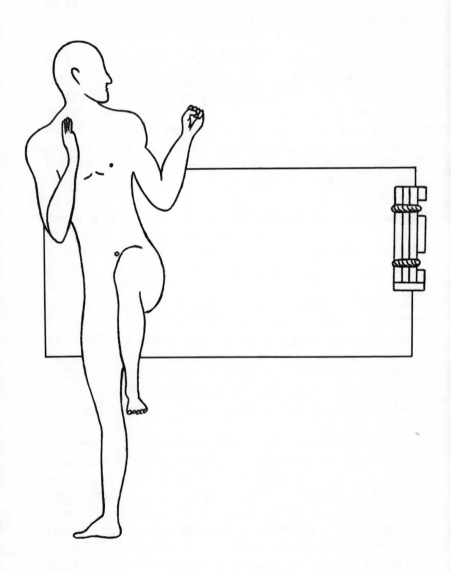

Figure 79

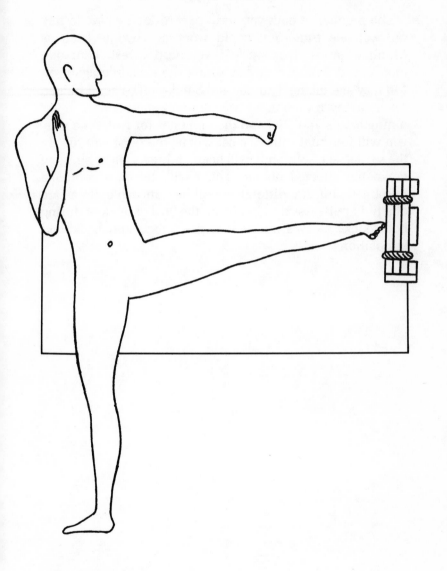

Figure 80

TRAINING SCHEDULES

The number of days you train per week may have to rely on available time. You could work a schedule such as Monday, hands; Tuesday, feet; Wednesday, rest; Thursday, hands; and Friday, feet, beginning the schedule again on Monday and taking Saturday and Sunday off. When I trained for breaking my schedule was six consecutive days, alternating hands and feet, and then one day for rest. As a rule, you will find that your first set will be the most painful. By the second set, your body will begin doing its job by shutting down the affected nerves. There will not be a complete numbness, but the difference will be noticeable. Be aware of a fluid puffiness developing on the heel of the foot during hook kicks as was advised in the punch and backhand annotations.

Chapter 7

Breaking

At this point you have seen eighty illustrations and have studied the necessary steps to prepare you for breaking. If you have trained properly and if you know you are ready to attempt your first break, then you should have already struck the boards or bricks you plan on breaking with a full-power blow without pain. If you are going to try a break on two boards with a punch, you should have already fastened the boards to your training block and hit them with a full-power blow. You should be confident that even if the boards do not break, you will not be injured from the impact. This same prerequisite should be applied to any object you plan on trying to break, whether with a weapon of the hands or the feet. Confidence is necessary; there must be no fear.

All of what you have read and seen thus far are elementary teachings from the Lian Shi kung-fu system. In this system there is a fundamental framework to all movements consisting of four elements: *Lian Li* (power), *Lian Su* (speed), *Lian Chin* (accuracy), and *Chiau Yuwn* (spirit). Power, the Lian Li element, has a physical source which comes from a trained body. Lian Su and Lian Chin also have a physical source which comes from a trained body. Chiau Yuwn means, literally, "joining the spirit," and this fourth element, which is nonphysical, must be united with the physical elements to have inner and outer unity of force in breaking or any other martial art techniques. Chiau Yuwn is difficult to teach, and I have found that it is often necessary to start a student across this bridge by giving him or her a point of focus. Not a physical point, but an emotional point. Just as many writers have been inspired to great works by the love of a mate or the tragedy of having lost one, it is helpful for the martial artist to have an emotional point of focus. To bring about anger is helpful and is a good start, but after a great many years of teaching and studying my students I have found that there is a single word and a corresponding attitude that transcends anger as a focal point. The word is *intent*. When a lioness runs down her prey and kills it, she is ferocious and purposeful in her attack, but as ferocious as she is, the lioness is not angry. She kills to eat and to feed her cubs, or for self-defense. You may one day have to fight with everything inside to survive. You would be fighting as hard and as fiercely as possible, but anger may not be present. So what would be? Intent! There would be a deliberate and purposeful desire to crush your aggressor, and not necessarily out of anger, but there would be intent. You might say that Chiau Yuwn is the will, a want channeled into the physical body but on an emotional plane, not a mental plane. What all this means in your breaking is that when you stand before the object to be broken, you must be completely committed to the task, not just physically and mentally, but emotionally as well. Your body is par for the task, and your mind has the desire to be successful in your attempt. Now you must get emotionally involved in your effort. Be it tears, a grunt, growl, or deafening scream, commit your emotions to the effort. When you add the Chiau Yuwn element to the three physical elements of Lian Li, Lian Su, and Lian Chin, you have internal as well as external powers working.

One last subject must be discussed before studying the actual breaking. Observe Figures 81 and 82. Because most of the breaking illustrations in this chapter involve a training partner holding the boards to be broken, let's take a quick

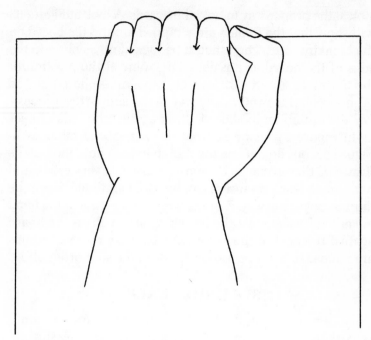

Figure 81

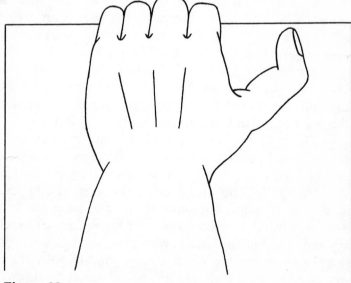

Figure 82

look at the proper way to hold the boards. A look at Figure 83 will show that the fingers are wrapped around the board on the breaking side. They should be tucked up as close to the edge of the board as possible. Look now at the position of the thumb in Figures 81 and 82. You can see here that the thumb is not involved in any way in the supportive process. Lay the thumb on the board either against the index finger as in Figure 81, or away from the rest of the hand as in Figure 82, but do not use the thumb to help hold the boards firm. The thumb can be broken or dislocated very easily, and with much less pressure it can be badly sprained. Keep the thumbs out of the way. Rest the board on the heel of the hand to keep it firm against the incoming strike. Press the board against the heel of the hand with the fingers. The thumbs are neither safe nor necessary to use in the supportive effort.

STRAIGHT PUNCH

Just as you measured off and set your stance for proximity in working on the training block, you must also measure off in breaking. An extended punch should penetrate its target by no less than two inches and up to eight inches. Observe Figures 83, 84, and 85. In Figure 83 the boards are being held at arm's length and at chest level. Never hold boards at face height. The boards will often break away from the grip and could be dangerous if they strike the face. The breaker in Figure 83 is set in a left forward stance with the left punch chambered. In Figure 84 the punch is extended to the point of contact, but notice that the arm is not locked out. In Figure 85 the punch is locked in the open position and has passed through the boards. When measuring your stance and depth of penetration, set yourself by the illustration in Figure 84. Think and decide before even setting your stance what it is you are going to do, and keep the four elements in mind. If upon impact the boards do not break and you do not feel any pain in your hand, change to a right forward stance and try again. Unless you are going for a heavy power break, it should not be necessary to support the punch with the stance, but with the opposite leg straight

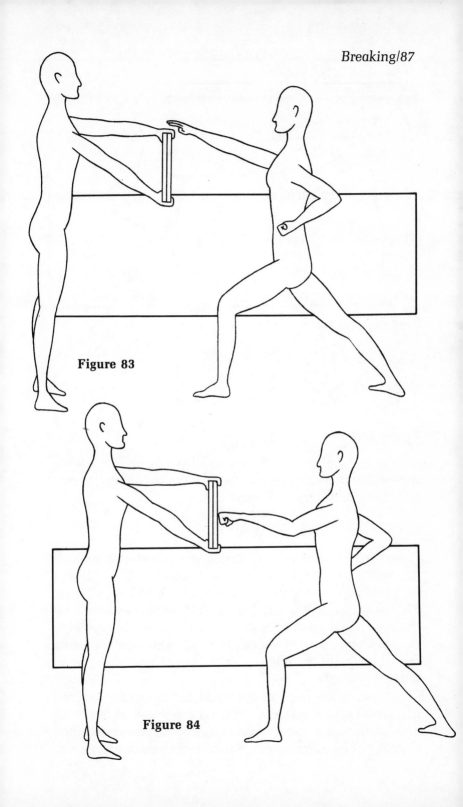

Figure 83

Figure 84

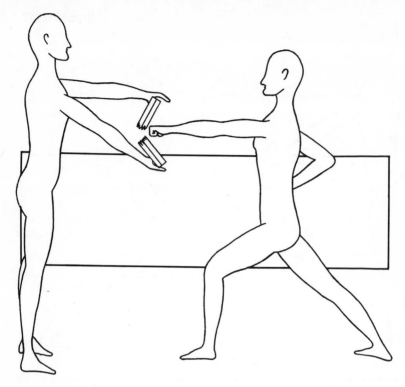

Figure 85

behind the punching arm you will have greater resistance
to negative impact force and have a more solid thrust to give
you more total power if needed.

BACKHAND

As you have been doing in the training process, set yourself
in a straddle stance, but measure your depth for two or more
inches of penetration into the boards. Looking at Figures 86,
87, and 88, you will notice that the training partner is holding
the boards at a distance slightly behind the person throwing
the backhand. This is necessary to keep you from striking
the boards with the forearm as the knuckles make contact
with the boards.

The stationary form of the backhand is strictly a speed
movement and will not have nearly the power of the other
hand strikes. Your expectations in terms of power therefore
should not be as great when performing the backhand as

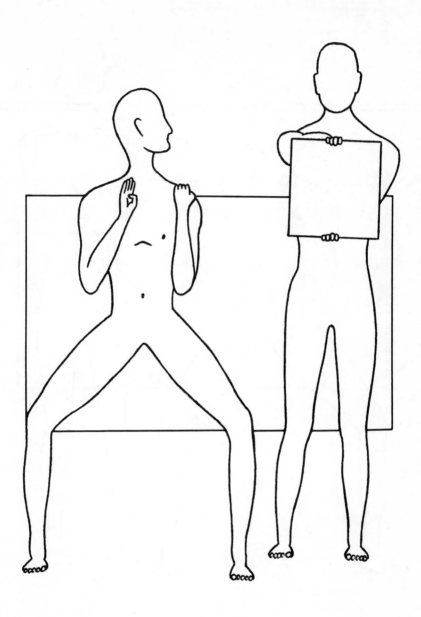

Figure 86

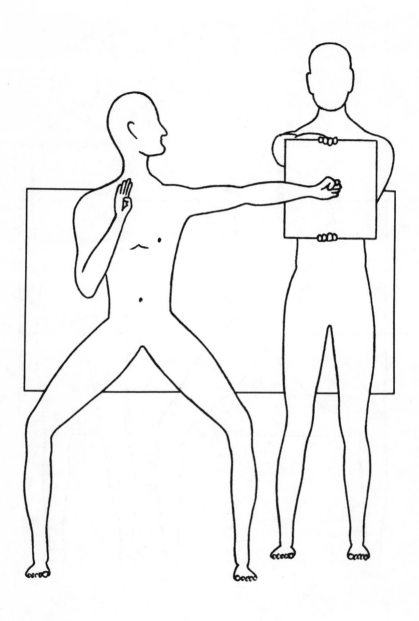

Figure 87

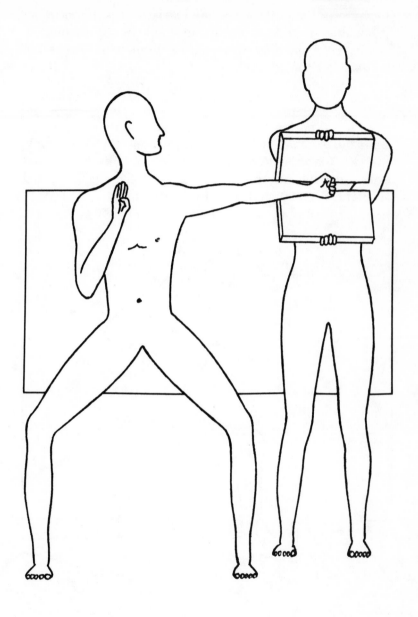

Figure 88

they are in the other three hand strikes. It is, however, an invaluable weapon in combat and should not be discounted. Again, keep the four elements in mind while preparing yourself for the attempt.

SUTO

As noted earlier in the text, the suto will develop much more quickly than the other hand weapons. If you are breaking two boards with a straight punch, it is likely that you will be capable of breaking two cement slabs, as illustrated in Figures 89, 90, and 91, with your suto.

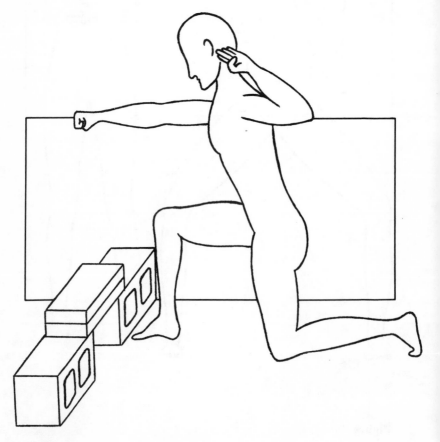

Figure 89

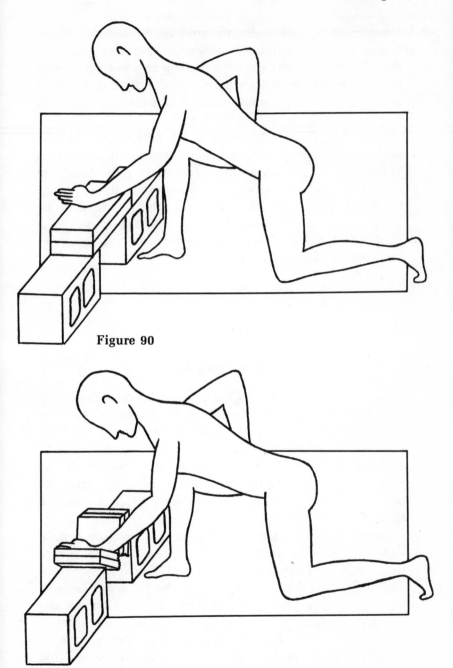

Figure 90

Figure 91

When we began training the suto, we discussed the location of the full chamber position for the suto. Figure 89 depicts that position. Because it is not safe to hold cement slabs for breaking, they are pictured here supported at each end by a standard cement block. A one-inch overlap onto the supporting blocks is sufficient.

Observing Figures 89, 90, and 91, notice first that the opposing hand begins extended outward and is chambered to the punching position on impact of the suto. Also note that the position of the body is different in all three illustrations. When cement blocks or bricks are being broken, the body weight should be used to maximize the power of the stroke. As these three illustrations demonstrate, the upper body should follow the stroke.

PALM STRIKE

The palm strike has no specific chamber position. It can be held in the form in which the suto is held, or it can be positioned as in Figure 92. Note here the positions of the upper body in Figures 93 and 94 as the movement progresses to the final break. Like the suto, the palm power will be increased by bringing the body weight with the strike. As discussed in the punch instructions, keep the four elements in mind.

Like the suto, the palm strike's power source utilizes centrifugal force as well as muscle and the technical structure of the movement. The potential for power is therefore very great. Your initial breaking attempts with the palm are likely to be successful if your hand is properly conditioned, but remember where you started in the conditioning process. Do not start with a hard breaking attempt. You can always make a second and third attempt according to how the first break affected your hand.

Figure 92

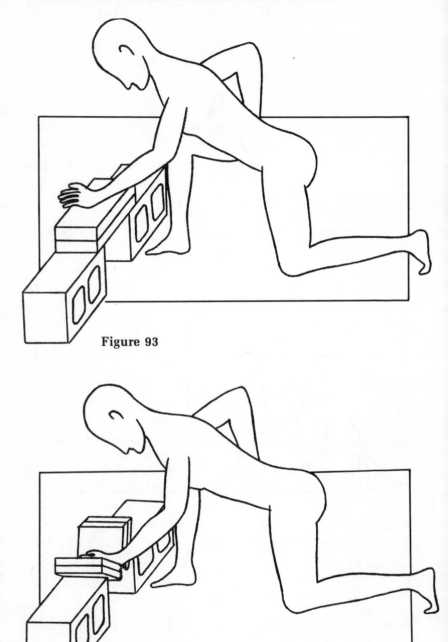

Figure 93

Figure 94

FRONT KICK

When we began training the breaking weapons, hands were worked one day, feet the next. Do not alter the sequence now. When you have fifteen or twenty breaking sessions under your belt, you will have enough experience and enough of an understanding of your body's capabilities and limitations to combine hand and foot breaking into one day. At this point, you will need all of your mental powers to maintain proper form to reduce the chances of injury. Set up a separate day for breaking with kicks.

Figures 95, 96, and 97 illustrate the sequence of breaking with the front kick. If you have trained according to the instructions given thus far, the form and technique are familiar to you here as they have been in all the breaking instructions in this chapter. The only difference is the increased penetration. Kicks should penetrate from two to twelve inches through a target, according to the width of the object itself. Looking at Figure 96, note that at contact with the boards, the kick is not locked into the open position. The

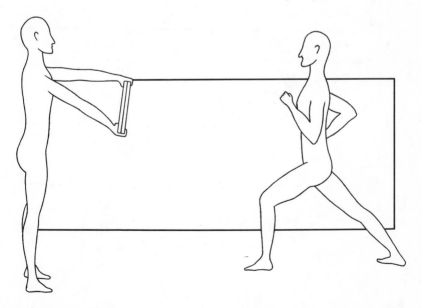

Figure 95

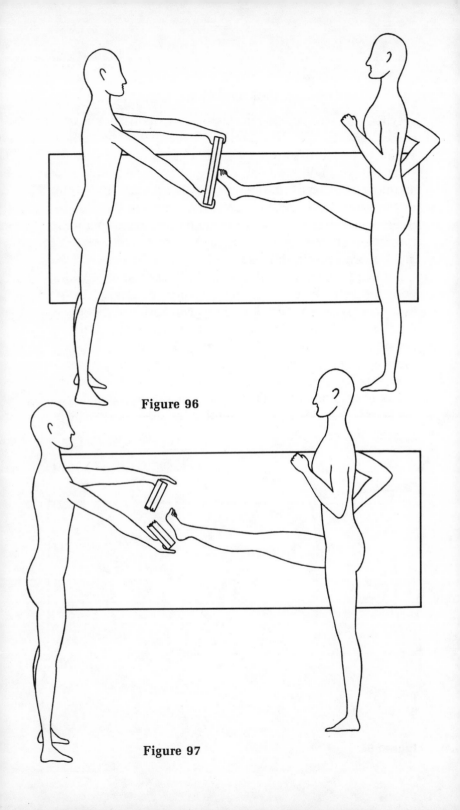

Figure 96

Figure 97

key is to lock *through* the target as depicted in Figure 97. Penetration is critical. All of the instructions discussed in the section on breaking with the hand apply here as well.

HOOK KICK

Your constant training for the hook kick will be seen in your breaking attempt. Balance will be a factor. You should have learned something very important from your breaking attempts with the hands. When you are training on a block, the positive impact force does not affect your balance. When you pass through a breaking object, however, that force may very well carry you forward and off balance if you overpower the object by a great percentage. For hand techniques, that

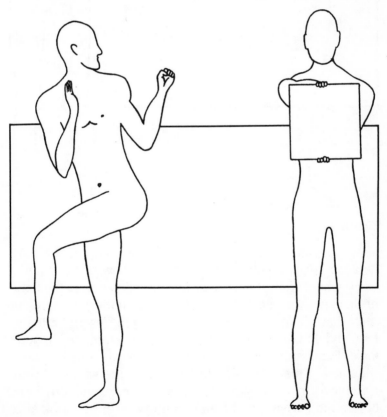

Figure 98

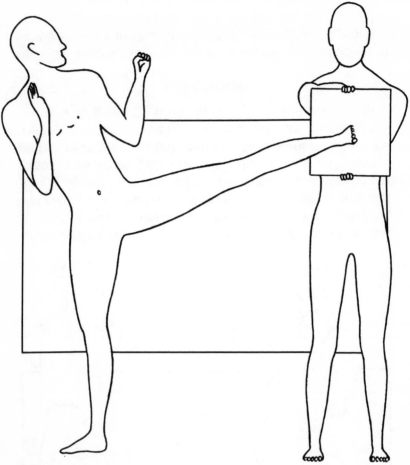

Figure 99

usually means nothing more than a slight loss of upper body balance and a resulting lift of the rear heel of the stance. For the hook kick, that may mean stumbling across the floor or losing your footing altogether and falling. Control is important. Channel your power through the leg and into the foot, and do not allow your body weight to be carried by your kick. Figures 98, 99, and 100 demonstrate the breaking sequence. This form should be exactly the same as your training form. Make several successful breaks with this form before improvising and trying to break with the hook kick out of a different stance or with an advancing movement.

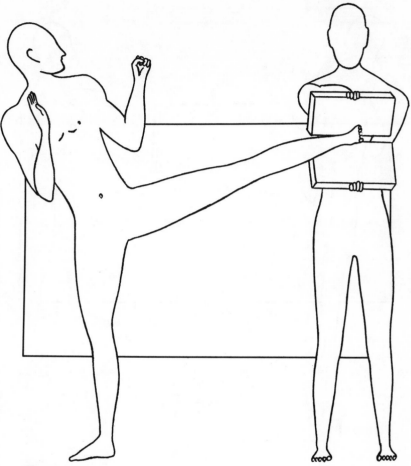

Figure 100

SIDE KICK

In Figures 101 through 103, the side kick is demonstrated in a breaking sequence. Again, your experience on the training block is going to bring you to a successful break. Like the hook kick, the side kick requires balance, but this is the only breaking technique discussed in this text that when unsuccessful will knock you off balance 90 percent of the time. Look at Figure 103. Picture the kick completely extended but the boards not broken. The power has to go somewhere, and there are two confined points of proximity. There will not be enough room to extend the kick if the boards do

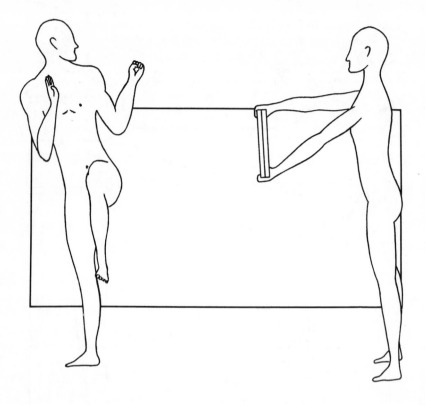

Figure 101

not break. Therefore, when the leg locks into the open position either the person holding the boards will be knocked
backward or the person throwing the kick will be forced
backward.

I recall attempting a break on eight one-inch boards with
a crossing advance side kick out of a straddle stance. When
I hit the boards, my kick locked out completely but the boards
did not break on the first attempt. The boards were fastened
to a wall-mounted breaking rack. The boards did not break,
the cement block wall did not move, and the rack was made
of angle iron and did not give. My final step with the supporting leg confined my body to a proximity to the target

that demanded six inches of penetration through the boards with my foot. When I locked out my leg, there was no room between my stance and the boards for the leg to open fully. As a result, I was shot backward two-thirds of the way across a twenty-four foot mat before I realized it. Be it one board or a hundred boards, if you do not pass through the target and the supporting structure of the target does not give, you will be forced backward. Expect this reaction.

The breaking sequences are all illustrated; you have the technical understanding necessary to develop your weapons. Your efforts and dedication are all that are required beyond this point.

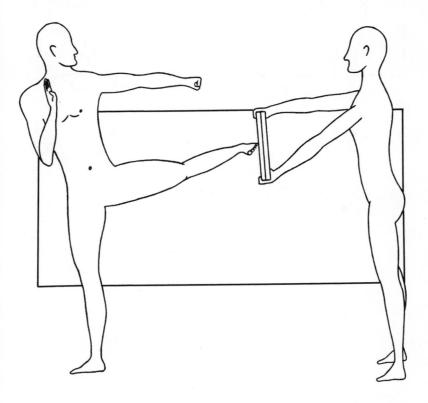

Figure 102

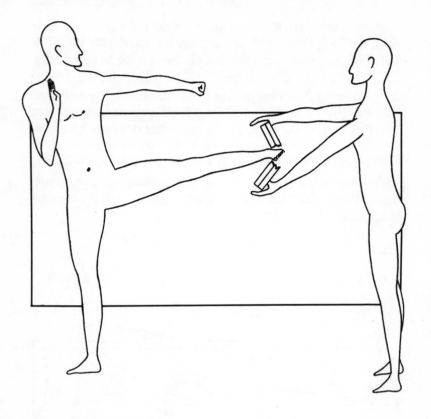

Figure 103